QUIZMASTER

The Royal Family

200 Questions in total!

Ginny Hill

"I declare before you all that my whole life, whether it be long or short, shall be devoted to your service and the service of our great imperial family to which we all belong."

Her Majesty Queen Elizabeth II

QUIZMASTER

Introduction

Welcome to Quizmaster, a series of quiz books based on themed questions.

Enjoy a wide range of interesting, fun and curious questions!

Use Quizmaster to challenge your knowledge or run your own quiz. Quizmaster books have handy hints for organizing quizzes and a sample answer sheet for you to use.

All answers have been checked and are given as accurately as possible at the time of publishing. If you disagree with an answer, please contact me at emailginnyhill@gmail.com. Thank you.

All the questions and answers to the 200 questions in this book are related to 'The Royal Family', with 20 theme-based rounds all about British Royalty.

Other quizzes from the Quizmaster series:

Music
Christmas
Food and Drink
Months of the Year
Scotland
USA
Seasons
Homes
Love
Colours
The Seaside

How to use Quizmaster Books

Quizmaster Books are separated into 3 sections for ease of use:

Section 1
This section consists of 20 quiz rounds, each with 10 questions. The answers for each round are on the following page. This enables the reader to complete each quiz round without seeing the answers.

Section 2
This section is ideal for people running their own quizzes with the questions and answers appearing on the same page. The questions are the same as those in Section 1.

Section 3
This section contains 10 helpful hints for anyone organizing their own quiz, plus a sample answer sheet.

Happy Quizzing!

"Your mind will answer most questions if you learn to relax and wait for the answer."

William S. Burroughs

Table of Contents

Introduction 3

How to use Quizmaster Books 5

Quizmaster Section 1: QUESTIONS 10

QUIZ 1: QUEEN ELIZABETH II 11
    ANSWERS 12

QUIZ 2: EARLY KINGS AND QUEENS OF ENGLAND 13
    ANSWERS 14

QUIZ 3: ROYAL WEDDINGS 15
    ANSWERS 16

QUIZ 4: THE COMMONWEALTH 17
    ANSWERS 18

QUIZ 5: HENRY VIII 19
    ANSWERS 20

QUIZ 6: ROYALS IN SPORT 21
    ANSWERS 22

QUIZ 7: ROYAL LITERATURE 23
    ANSWERS 24

QUIZ 8: THE ELIZABETHAN ERA 25
    ANSWERS 26

QUIZ 9: THE ROYAL HOUSEHOLDS 27
    ANSWERS 28

QUIZ 10: ROYAL MUSIC 29
    ANSWERS 30

QUIZ 11: THE EDWARDIAN ERA 31
    ANSWERS 32

QUIZ 12: BY ROYAL APPOINTMENT 33
    ANSWERS 34

QUIZ 13: ROYAL ANIMALS	35
ANSWERS	36
QUIZ 14: ROYAL VEHICLES	37
ANSWERS	38
QUIZ 15: QUEEN VICTORIA	39
ANSWERS	40
QUIZ 16: STATE VISITS	41
ANSWERS	42
QUIZ 17: ROYAL FOOD	43
ANSWERS	44
QUIZ 18: BRITISH STAMPS	45
ANSWERS	46
QUIZ 19: ROYAL CASTLES AND PALACES	47
ANSWERS	48
QUIZ 20: THE REIGN OF ELIZABETH II	49
ANSWERS	50
Quizmaster Section 2: Questions with Answers	51
QUIZ 1: QUEEN ELIZABETH II	52
QUIZ 2: EARLY KINGS AND QUEENS OF ENGLAND	53
QUIZ 3: ROYAL WEDDINGS	54
QUIZ 4: THE COMMONWEALTH	55
QUIZ 5: HENRY VIII	56
QUIZ 6: ROYALS IN SPORT	57
QUIZ 7: ROYAL LITERATURE	58
QUIZ 8: THE ELIZABETHAN ERA	59
QUIZ 9: THE ROYAL HOUSEHOLDS	60
QUIZ 10: ROYAL MUSIC	61
QUIZ 11: THE EDWARDIAN ERA	62
QUIZ 12: BY ROYAL APPOINTMENT	63

QUIZ 13: ROYAL ANIMALS 64

QUIZ 14: ROYAL VEHICLES 65

QUIZ 15: QUEEN VICTORIA 66

QUIZ 16: STATE VISITS 67

QUIZ 17: ROYAL FOOD...68

QUIZ 18: BRITISH STAMPS 69

QUIZ 19: ROYAL CASTLES AND PALACES 70

QUIZ 20: THE REIGN OF ELIZABETH II 71

Quizmaster Section 3: BE YOUR OWN QUIZMASTER!..................72
    Quizmaster Helpful Hints..73

Quizmaster Sample Answer Sheet 75

THANKS..76

MORE TITLES BY GINNY HILL 77

Quizmaster Section 1: QUESTIONS

Work your way through a wide range of questions all based on 'Royalty'. Test your knowledge on a range of questions from Royal castles and palaces, vehicles and food to Royal music, weddings and animals!

QUIZ 1: QUEEN ELIZABETH II

A range of questions about Her Majesty, Queen Elizabeth II.

1. In which country was Elizabeth staying when she became Queen of England?

2. On which date is the Queen's real birthday?

3. When she is in residence in London, who does the Queen meet every Tuesday?

4. From a military base in 1976, the Queen sent her first *what*?

5. Apart from 1969, what has the Queen broadcasted to the nation every year?

6. Which ceremony takes place annually to celebrate the Queen's official birthday?

7. Who was the actor that appeared alongside the Queen and her corgis in a James Bond sketch for the opening of the Olympic Games in London, 2012?

8. What annual summer event does the Queen hold at Buckingham Palace and the Palace of Holyroodhouse?

9. From which country did the gold come from for the Queen's wedding ring?

10. Who, of the Queen's four children, was the first child to be born to a reigning monarch since Victorian times?

QUIZ 1: QUEEN ELIZABETH II

ANSWERS

1. Kenya

2. 21st April

3. British Prime Minister

4. Email

5. Christmas Message

6. Trooping the Colour

7. Daniel Craig

8. Garden Parties

9. Wales

10. Prince Andrew

QUIZ 2: EARLY KINGS AND QUEENS OF ENGLAND

Test your knowledge on early reigns.

1. The Magna Carta was signed by which king on 15th June 1215?

2. Which animal, presented to Henry III by the King of Norway, was taken daily to the River Thames to catch fish and have a swim?

3. Regarding currency, what did Henry VII become the first king to do?

4. Who is the only King of England to be called 'Great'?

5. Who reigned for just 9 days before being deposed in 1553?

6. What was forbidden to be worn in Parliament after a statute agreed by Edward II in 1313?

7. Which animal did James I keep in St. James Park?

8. Which king was on the throne at the time of the Great Fire of London in 1666?

9. What did the fountains contain that were opened across London to celebrate the coronation of Richard II?

10. Which Henry became king at 9 months of age?

QUIZ 2: EARLY KINGS AND QUEENS OF ENGLAND

ANSWERS

1. John

2. Polar Bear

3. Have his portrait stamped on coins

4. Alfred

5. Lady Jane Grey

6. Armour

7. Elephant

8. Charles II

9. Wine

10. Henry VI

QUIZ 3: ROYAL WEDDINGS

Which member of the Royal Family did these people marry?

1. Catherine Elizabeth Middleton

2. Lieutenant Philip Mountbatten

3. Angus Ogilvy

4. Timothy James Hamilton Lawrence

5. Camilla Parker Bowles

6. Anthony Charles Armstrong-Jones

7. Autumn Kelly

8. Baroness Marie Christine von Reibnitz

9. Sophie Helen Rhys-Jones

10. Alice Douglas-Montague-Scott

QUIZ 3: ROYAL WEDDINGS

ANSWERS

1. Prince William
2. Queen Elizabeth II
3. Princess Alexandra of Kent
4. Princess Anne
5. Prince Charles
6. Princess Margaret
7. Peter Phillips
8. Prince Michael of Kent
9. Prince Edward
10. Prince Henry, Duke of Gloucester

QUIZ 4: THE COMMONWEALTH

Answer these varied questions about 'The Commonwealth of Nations'.

1. Which 'tradition' first began on a tour of Australia and New Zealand in 1970?

2. When visiting Tonga in 1953, which royal reptile did the Queen meet during her stay?

3. First held at Hamilton, Canada in 1930, what modern name is given to the multi-sport event that has been held every four years since, apart from during World War 2?

4. The smallest nation in the Commonwealth by population is Nauru. Which is the largest nation by population?

5. On which Commonwealth island did the Queen and Prince Philip live during 1949–51 when the Duke was serving in the Royal Navy?

6. Which Commonwealth state was the first to have a female prime minister?

7. What is celebrated annually across the Commonwealth on the second Monday of March?

8. Why did the Queen have to interrupt a tour of Australia and Indonesia and return to Britain in 1974?

9. When visiting Fiji, the Queen has always been given a gift of a tooth from which mammal?

10. Which UNESCO World Heritage Centre did the Queen open during a tour to Australia in 1973?

QUIZ 4: THE COMMONWEALTH

ANSWERS

1. Royal Walkabout

2. Royal Tortoise

3. Commonwealth Games

4. India

5. Malta

6. Sri Lanka

7. Commonwealth Day

8. A snap election was called

9. Whale

10. Sydney Opera House

QUIZ 5: HENRY VIII

Test your knowledge of Henry VIII.

1. Who was Henry VIII's first wife?

2. At what age did Henry VIII become king?

3. Henry VIII became successor to the throne after his older brother died. What was his brother's name?

4. Which religious title was bestowed on Henry VIII by the Pope and was never relinquished when Henry broke away from Rome?

5. English and Latin were two of three languages spoken by Henry VIII. Name the third language.

6. Henry VIII imposed a tax on what part of the body, although he himself was exempt from the rule?

7. Lasting 6 months and 3 days before it was annulled, to whom was Henry VIII married for the shortest time?

8. Which book did Henry VIII authorise for reading out loud in church?

9. Shipbuilding was an important investment for Henry VIII. Which boat did he name after his sister?

10. Who succeeded Henry VIII to the throne?

QUIZ 5: HENRY VIII

ANSWERS

1. Catherine of Aragon
2. 17 Years
3. Arthur
4. Defender of the Faith
5. French
6. Beards
7. Anne of Cleves
8. (Great) Bible
9. Mary Rose
10. Edward VI

QUIZ 6: ROYALS IN SPORT

Questions on a range of royal sporting activities.

1. Who was the first member of the Royal Family to participate in the Olympic Games?

2. The racing colours of Queen Elizabeth II are purple and red with gold braiding. What colour is the cap?

3. Which member of the Royal Family instigated the Invictus Games?

4. Who became President of the All England Lawn Tennis and Croquet Club in 1969?

5. Sometimes called the "sport of kings", which racquet sport did Henry VIII play at Hampton Palace?

6. Which June sporting event was started by Queen Anne in 1711 and is attended every year by members of the Royal Family?

7. Which Royal Family member was a captain of the England rugby team?

8. What was given to the Royal Family in 1886, starting a royal interest in this recreational sport?

9. Who became President of the Football Association in May 2006?

10. Which member of the Royal Family won a Silver medal at the 2012 Olympic Games in London?

QUIZ 6: ROYALS IN SPORT

ANSWERS

1. Princess Anne

2. Black with a Gold Fringe

3. Prince Harry

4. Prince Michael, Duke of Kent

5. Real Tennis

6. Royal Ascot

7. Mike Tindall

8. Racing Pigeons

9. Prince William

10. Zara Phillips

QUIZ 7: ROYAL LITERATURE

*Name the royal authors of these published books.
The date of publication is in brackets.*

1. "The Old Man of Lochnagar" (1980)

2. "Elizabeth R: A Photographic Celebration of 40 Years" (1991)

3. "The Defence of the Seven Sacraments" (1521)

4. "Budgie the Little Helicopter" (1995)

5. "Harmony: A New Way of Looking at Our World" (2010)

6. "The Adventures of Alice Laselles" (Written 1829/Published 2015)

7. "Competition Carriage Driving" (1982)

8. "Agnes Sorel: Mistress of Beauty" (2014)

9. "Daemonology" (1597)

10. "The Environmental Revolution" (1978)

QUIZ 7: ROYAL LITERATURE

ANSWERS

1. Prince Charles
2. Earl of Lichfield
3. Henry VIII
4. Duchess of York
5. Prince Charles
6. Queen Victoria
7. Prince Philip
8. Princess Michael of Kent
9. King James VI of Scotland
10. Prince Philip

QUIZ 8: THE ELIZABETHAN ERA

Test your knowledge of events during the reign of Elizabeth I.

1. Henry VIII was the father of Elizabeth I. Who was her mother?

2. Which naval fleet was defeated by the English in 1588?

3. During the Elizabethan era the government was made up of the monarch, parliament and which other council?

4. Sir Walter Raleigh is famed for bringing which vegetable back to Europe from his explorations?

5. Which Elizabethan playhouse, situated on the River Thames, was associated with William Shakespeare?

6. In 1562, Elizabeth I was very ill from which infectious disease?

7. Which local English language could Elizabeth I speak, a language that is still spoken by about 2,000 people?

8. What did over 20,000 people in London die from in 1563?

9. Elizabethan laws dictated what clothes people could wear. What were only Royal people allowed to wear on their cuffs?

10. Who was the first Englishman to circumnavigate the globe on a ship called "The Golden Hind"?

QUIZ 8: THE ELIZABETHAN ERA

ANSWERS

1. Anne Boleyn
2. Spanish Armada
3. Privy Council
4. Potato
5. The Globe
6. Smallpox
7. Cornish
8. Bubonic Plague/The Black Death
9. Ermine Fur
10. Sir Francis Drake

QUIZ 9: THE ROYAL HOUSEHOLDS

These questions are about the Royal Households who are responsible for supporting members of the Royal Family.
Select your answer from the multiple-choice options.

1. The Lord Steward and the Lord Chamberlain are two of the three Great Officers of the Household. Who is the third Officer?
    Prime Minister/Master of the Horse/Private Secretary

2. Which member of the Royal Household can be heard at 9.00 am every morning?
    Master of the Household/Household Dog Walker/Queen's Piper

3. Who looks after the Queen's personal finances?
    Keeper of the Privy Purse/Chancellor of the Exchequer/Bank Manager

4. Apart from English, in which language might the Queen's approval be given for bills of Parliament?
    Latin/French/Spanish

5. Approximately, how many phone calls did the Royal Household receive in 2017?
    300,000/500,000/700,000

6. What is the Crown Equerry responsible for looking after?
    Royal Mews/Kensington Palace/Palace Gardens

7. In 2017, approximately how many people attended Garden Parties hosted by the Queen?
    30,000/50,000/70,000

8. Approximately, how many offices are there in Buckingham Palace?
    52/72/92

9. Which document is issued every day by the Royal Household?
    News Bulletin/Court Circular/Staffing List

10. During every State Opening of Parliament, who is taken hostage by the Royal Household?
    A Judge/An MP/A Bishop

QUIZ 9: THE ROYAL HOUSEHOLDS

ANSWERS

1. Master of the Horse

2. Queen's Piper

3. Keeper of the Privy Purse

4. French

5. 700,000

6. Royal Mews

7. 50,000

8. 92

9. Court Circular

10. An MP

QUIZ 10: ROYAL MUSIC

Questions linked to royalty and music.

1. Who wrote the "Music for the Royal Fireworks"?

2. Which patriotic song was first performed publicly in 1745?

3. The composer of "Pomp and Circumstance" became "Master of the King's Music" in 1924. Who was he?

4. Which London concert venue was dedicated to a prince following his death?

5. In 2000, Prince Charles revived the appointment of which musician to the Royal Court?

6. According to the nursery rhyme, who "marched his men to the top of the hill and he marched them down again"?

7. Opened in 1892, which performing arts venue in Covent Garden was formerly a theatre?

8. Who played his guitar on the roof of Buckingham Palace as part of the Golden Jubilee celebrations in 2002?

9. What did the Queen receive following the recording sales of "Party At The Palace", the first member of the Royal Family to be given this music honour?

10. The music for which planet from Holst's "The Planets" was used at the coronation of Queen Elizabeth II and is also the tune for the hymn "I Vow to Thee, My Country?"

QUIZ 10: ROYAL MUSIC

ANSWERS

1. Handel

2. National Anthem

3. Edward Elgar

4. Albert Hall

5. Harpist

6. The Grand Old Duke of York

7. Royal Opera House

8. Brian May

9. Gold Disc

10. Jupiter

QUIZ 11: THE EDWARDIAN ERA

Each question is about an event that occurred during the Edwardian era.

1. In which year did Edward VII become king?

2. In 1908, which sporting event was held in London?

3. Who, with her daughters, founded the Women's Social and Political Union in 1902?

4. Name the successful children's book written by Beatrix Potter and published by Frederick Warne & Co. in 1902.

5. Which shopkeeper opened a store in Oxford Street in 1909, and put cosmetics on open display for the first time?

6. French aviator, Louis Blériot, invented an aircraft that was used to successfully cross which body of water for the first time in 1909?

7. Which playwright wrote "Man and Superman" and "Pygmalion" during the Edwardian era?

8. What prizes, still awarded today, were presented for the first time in 1901 for work in the fields of literature, medicine, physics, chemistry and peace?

9. Who, in 1905, proposed a "Theory of Relativity"?

10. Which part of the world was reached for the first time by explorer Roald Amundsen in 1911?

QUIZ 11: THE EDWARDIAN ERA

ANSWERS

1. 1901

2. Summer Olympic Games

3. Emmeline Pankhurst

4. The Tale of Peter Rabbit

5. Gordon Selfridge

6. English Channel

7. George Bernard Shaw

8. Nobel Prizes

9. Albert Einstein

10. South Pole

QUIZ 12: BY ROYAL APPOINTMENT

Answer these questions about Royal Warrants, given in recognition of those who have supplied goods or services to the Royal Household.

1. What is the minimum length of time a trader has to supply goods or services to the Royal Household before being considered for a Royal Warrant?

2. A Royal Warrant can be granted by the Queen, the Duke of Edinburgh and which other Royal member?

3. Which dairy product is associated with Royal Warrant holders "Paxton and Whitfield"?

4. Approximately, how many suppliers held Royal Warrants in 2017?

5. Which purveyor of baked beans and tomato ketchup has a Royal Warrant?

6. What type of hat did Lock & Co., hat suppliers to the Royal Household, create?

7. After how many years does a Royal Warrant have to be renewed?

8. Barrow & Gale, Royal Warrant Holders, produce special purses traditionally given out by the Queen just before Easter Sunday. What name is given to the silver coins put into the purses?

9. In the 18th century the "Royal Bug-Taker" was responsible for getting rid of what type of bug?

10. What is the name of the Piccadilly grocery store that is often referred to as the "Queen's grocer"?

QUIZ 12: BY ROYAL APPOINTMENT

ANSWERS

1. 5 Years
2. Prince of Wales
3. Cheese
4. 800
5. Heinz
6. Bowler Hat
7. 5 Years
8. Maundy Money
9. Bed Bugs
10. Fortnum and Mason

QUIZ 13: ROYAL ANIMALS

Questions about the Royal Family and their love of animals.

1. What type of dog was created by the Queen?

2. The Queen, together with the Worshipful Company of Vintners and the Worshipful Company of Dyers, own all British swans. What is the name of the annual ceremony to count the swans on the River Thames?

3. Which animals reside in the main hall at Balmoral Castle?

4. What was the name of the horse with which Zara Philips won a number of equestrian gold medals?

5. Which exotic animal was given to the Queen and Princess Margaret by their second cousin, Lord Mountbatten?

6. Belonging to the Duke and Duchess of Cambridge, what breed of dog is "Lupo"?

7. The term "Fishes Royal" refers to ownership by the Queen of any whale, porpoise, dolphin or sturgeon that is caught or lands within how many miles of the British coastline?

8. The Queen's horse, "Estimate" won the Ascot Gold Cup in 2013. As the Queen normally presents the Cup, who did the honours?

9. In 1979, Prince Charles came third in a race at the Royal International Horse Show. What type of animal was he riding?

10. Which animal is being reinstituted on the Balmoral estate?

QUIZ 13: ROYAL ANIMALS

ANSWERS

1. Dorgi

2. Swan Upping

3. Bats

4. Toytown

5. Chameleon

6. Cocker Spaniel

7. 3 Miles

8. Prince Andrew, Duke of York

9. Camel

10. Red Squirrel

QUIZ 14: ROYAL VEHICLES

How does the Royal Family travel around?

1. What is the name of the boat that was often used by the Royal Family for both State visits and for family holidays?

2. The Queen is the only person in Britain who is not required to have a driving licence. What else is not needed on any car that the Queen drives?

3. On a State visit to Tuvalu, the Queen and Prince Philip travelled on what kind of water-craft?

4. Launched in 2014, what name has been given to the largest aircraft carrier belonging to the Royal Navy?

5. Which vehicle did Prince Philip buy in 1999 and has been used to transport the Prince around London?

6. Who was the first British monarch to travel by train?

7. During World War II, the Queen joined the Women's Auxillary Territorial Service and trained as a mechanic and driver of which army vehicle?

8. Where is the Queen's collection of cars stored?

9. In 1939, which transport system did the Queen and her sister Princess Margaret use for the first time?

10. What vehicle did the Queen use for travelling to Westminster Abbey for her coronation?

QUIZ 14: ROYAL VEHICLES

ANSWERS

1. Royal Yacht Britannia

2. Number Plate

3. Canoe

4. HMS Queen Elizabeth

5. London Taxi Cab/Metrocab

6. Queen Victoria

7. Military Truck

8. Royal Mews, Buckingham Palace

9. London Underground

10. Gold State Coach

QUIZ 15: QUEEN VICTORIA

A variety of questions on the life of Queen Victoria.

1. How many children did Queen Victoria and Prince Albert have?

2. "The Works of Industry of All Nations" were displayed in Hyde Park for almost six months in 1851. What was the occasion called?

3. At what age did Victoria become Queen of the United Kingdom?

4. What type of toy did Queen Victoria make as a child?

5. Which medal was introduced in 1856 to reward acts of courage during the Crimean War, and remains the highest British accolade of bravery today?

6. What was Queen Victoria's first name?

7. Queen Victoria presented a gift made from the timbers of HMS Resolute to President Rutherford B. Hayes. It has been used in the Oval Office by many US Presidents. What was the gift?

8. Which object did Queen Victoria possess that was bulletproof and lined with chainmail?

9. What did Queen Victoria wear on her wedding day that set a trend for brides that still exists today?

10. Queen Victoria was the first British monarch to sit for what sort of picture?

QUIZ 15: QUEEN VICTORIA

ANSWERS

1. 9

2. The Great Exhibition/Crystal Palace Exhibition

3. 18 Years

4. Peg Dolls

5. Victoria Cross

6. Alexandrina

7. Desk

8. Umbrella

9. White Wedding Dress

10. Photograph

QUIZ 16: STATE VISITS

Her Majesty Queen Elizabeth II has undertaken many state visits, both as a host and as a visitor to other countries. These questions are about state visits, both home and abroad.

1. What does the Queen not need when travelling abroad?

2. During a State visit in 1982, which American President did the Queen go horse riding with through Windsor Park?

3. Which country has been visited the most times by the Queen?

4. In 1983, which 'crooner' organised a royal tribute on the sound stage at 20th Century Fox in Hollywood?

5. Which was the first country that the Queen made a State visit to?

6. On a 1994 tour, where did the Queen watch the Bolshoi Ballet perform "Giselle"?

7. In 1986, the Queen became the first British monarch to visit which country?

8. During a tour of Brazil in 1968, which footballer impressed the Queen when she watched a match at the Maracanã Stadium?

9. King Bhumipol and Queen Sirikit made a State visit to the United Kingdom in 1960. Which country were they from?

10. In 1990, part of a state visit was a walk along a wooden pathway looking at hot springs and other geothermal activity. Which country was the Queen visiting?

QUIZ 16: STATE VISITS

ANSWERS

1. Passport
2. Ronald Reagan
3. Canada
4. Frank Sinatra
5. Norway
6. Moscow
7. China
8. Pelé
9. Thailand
10. Iceland

QUIZ 17: ROYAL FOOD

A variety of questions linking royalty and food.

1. Chicken, herbs, spices and mayonnaise are the main ingredients for a dish created in 1953. Name the recipe.

2. Which gift does the Queen customarily give to staff members at Christmas?

3. Eggs, butter, sugar and flour are used to make this layered cake which has jam in the middle. Name the cake.

4. What variety of potato is named after a monarch?

5. Which member of the Royal Family had a cider apple named after him on his 21st birthday?

6. Gingerbread and marchpane, a product similar to marzipan, were two favourite sugary treats during the reign of which British monarch?

7. In which Scandinavian country did the Queen eat smoked reindeer at a state banquet?

8. Name the pink and yellow cake that is covered in marzipan.

9. Which popular bread-based food is believed to have been named after an Italian queen?

10. What flavour is "Queen Mother's cake"?

QUIZ 17: ROYAL FOOD

ANSWERS

1. Coronation Chicken

2. Christmas Pudding

3. Victoria Sponge/Sandwich

4. King Edward

5. Prince William

6. Elizabeth I

7. Finland

8. Battenburg

9. Pizza Margherita

10. Chocolate

QUIZ 18: BRITISH STAMPS

The present day postal service has Royal roots.
Test your knowledge of British mail.

1. The Penny Black was the world's first adhesive stamp. The head of which king or queen is on the Penny Black?

2. Which English monarch introduced the Royal Mail?

3. What was the highest value stamp ever issued in Britain?

4. Which way does the Queen's head face on postage stamps?

5. What is different about British stamps from all other postage stamps in the world?

6. Where would you find the "Court Post Office"?

7. Who was the first non-royal to appear on UK postage stamps as a commemoration for the 400th anniversary of his birthday?

8. A miniature silhouette of the monarch's head appears on all UK stamps. What appears, in relation to the monarch, on UK post boxes?

9. What name is given to stamp collecting?

10. As one of the commemorative stamps for the Queen's 90th birthday, which member of the Royal Family appeared on a postage stamp at the age of 2 years?

QUIZ 18: BRITISH STAMPS

ANSWERS

1. Queen Victoria

2. Henry VIII

3. £5

4. To the left

5. Do not have the name of the country on them

6. Buckingham Palace

7. William Shakespeare

8. Monarch's Initials

9. Philately

10. Prince George

QUIZ 19: ROYAL CASTLES AND PALACES

Questions about Royal residences.

1. Acquired by George III in 1761, which building is the official London residence of the Queen?

2. In which part of the United Kingdom is the Queen's official residence of Hillsborough Castle?

3. Where was the childhood home of Elizabeth, the Queen Mother, and birthplace of Princess Margaret?

4. Osborne House was a former Royal residence of Queen Victoria. On which island can it be found?

5. The cast of which West End show performed at Windsor Castle during a state visit by President Jacques Chirac?

6. Which palace was given to Henry VIII as a gift from Cardinal Wolsey?

7. In London, where is the official residence of the Prince of Wales?

8. Which castle is frequented by the Royal Family for summer holidays?

9. Henry VIII was born in the Palace of Placentia, as was Queen Elizabeth I. In which Royal London borough is the Palace of Placentia?

10. What is the name of the country house in Norfolk where the Royal Family traditionally spends Christmas?

QUIZ 19: ROYAL CASTLES AND PALACES

ANSWERS

1. Buckingham Palace

2. Northern Ireland

3. Glamis Castle

4. Isle of Wight

5. Les Misérables

6. Hampton Court Palace

7. Clarence House

8. Balmoral

9. Greenwich

10. Sandringham House

QUIZ 20: THE REIGN OF ELIZABETH II

Her Majesty, Queen Elizabeth II has been on the throne for over 60 years. These questions are on events that have occurred during that time.

1. Who broke the four-minute mile barrier in 1954?

2. Which car appeared for the first time in 1959?

3. What trophy did an English sports team win in 1966?

4. What financial change was launched in the UK in 1971?

5. In 1977, which horse won the Grand National for the third time?

6. On 1st January, 1985, which electronic device was used publicly for the first time by Ernie Wise?

7. What did Tim Berniers-Lee invent in 1989?

8. What linked England and France in 1994?

9. How old was the Queen Mother on 4th August, 2000?

10. Which anniversary did the Queen celebrate on 7th February, 2017?

QUIZ 20: THE REIGN OF ELIZABETH II

ANSWERS

1. Roger Banister

2. Austin Mini

3. Football World Cup

4. Decimal Currency

5. Red Rum

6. Mobile Phone

7. World Wide Web

8. Channel Tunnel

9. 100 Years

10. Sapphire Jubilee (65 Years as Monarch)

Quizmaster Section 2: Questions with Answers

Ideal for Quizmasters to use!

QUIZ 1: QUEEN ELIZABETH II

A range of questions about Her Majesty, Queen Elizabeth II.

1. In which country was Elizabeth staying when she became Queen of England?

   Kenya

2. On which date is the Queen's real birthday?

   21st April

3. When she is in residence in London, who does the Queen meet every Tuesday?

   British Prime Minister

4. From a military base in 1976, the Queen sent her first *what*?

   Email

5. Apart from 1969, what has the Queen broadcasted to the nation every year?

   Christmas Message

6. Which ceremony takes place annually to celebrate the Queen's official birthday?

   Trooping the Colour

7. Who was the actor that appeared alongside the Queen and her corgis in a James Bond sketch for the opening of the Olympic Games in London, 2012?

   Daniel Craig

8. What annual summer event does the Queen hold at Buckingham Palace and the Palace of Holyroodhouse?

   Garden Parties

9. From which country did the gold come from for the Queen's wedding ring?

   Wales

10. Who, of the Queen's four children, was the first child to be born to a reigning monarch since Victorian times?

    Prince Andrew

QUIZ 2: EARLY KINGS AND QUEENS OF ENGLAND

Test your knowledge on early reigns.

1. The Magna Carta was signed by which king on 15th June 1215?

   John

2. Which animal, presented to Henry III by the King of Norway, was taken daily to the River Thames to catch fish and have a swim?

   Polar Bear

3. Regarding currency, what did Henry VII become the first king to do?

   Have his portrait stamped on coins

4. Who is the only King of England to be called 'Great'?

   Alfred

5. Who reigned for just 9 days before being deposed in 1553?

   Lady Jane Grey

6. What was forbidden to be worn in Parliament after a statute agreed by Edward II in 1313?

   Armour

7. Which animal did James I keep in St. James Park?

   Elephant

8. Which king was on the throne at the time of the Great Fire of London in 1666?

   Charles II

9. What did the fountains contain that were opened across London to celebrate the coronation of Richard II?

   Wine

10. Which Henry became king at 9 months of age?

    Henry VI

QUIZ 3: ROYAL WEDDINGS

Which member of the Royal Family did these people marry?

1. Catherine Elizabeth Middleton

    Prince William

2. Lieutenant Philip Mountbatten

    Queen Elizabeth II

3. Angus Ogilvy

    Princess Alexandra of Kent

4. Timothy James Hamilton Lawrence

    Princess Anne

5. Camilla Parker Bowles

    Prince Charles

6. Anthony Charles Armstrong-Jones

    Princess Margaret

7. Autumn Kelly

    Peter Phillips

8. Baroness Marie Christine von Reibnitz

    Prince Michael of Kent

9. Sophie Helen Rhys-Jones

    Prince Edward

10. Alice Douglas-Montague-Scott

    Prince Henry, Duke of Gloucester

QUIZ 4: THE COMMONWEALTH

Answer these varied questions about 'The Commonwealth of Nations'.

1. Which 'tradition' first began on a tour of Australia and New Zealand in 1970?

    Royal Walkabout

2. When visiting Tonga in 1953, which royal reptile did the Queen meet during her stay?

    Royal Tortoise

3. First held at Hamilton, Canada in 1930, what modern name is given to the multi-sport event that has been held every four years since, apart from during World War 2?

    Commonwealth Games

4. The smallest nation in the Commonwealth by population is Nauru. Which is the largest nation by population?

    India

5. On which Commonwealth island did the Queen and Prince Philip live during 1949–51 when the Duke was serving in the Royal Navy?

    Malta

6. Which Commonwealth state was the first to have a female prime minister?

    Sri Lanka

7. What is celebrated annually across the Commonwealth on the second Monday of March?

    Commonwealth Day

8. Why did the Queen have to interrupt a tour of Australia and Indonesia and return to Britain in 1974?

    A snap election was called

9. When visiting Fiji, the Queen has always been given a gift of a tooth from which mammal?

    Whale

10. Which UNESCO World Heritage Centre did the Queen open during a tour to Australia in 1973?

    Sydney Opera House

QUIZ 5: HENRY VIII

Test your knowledge of Henry VIII.

1. Who was Henry VIII's first wife?

   Catherine of Aragon

2. At what age did Henry VIII become king?

   17 Years

3. Henry VIII became successor to the throne after his older brother died. What was his brother's name?

   Arthur

4. Which religious title was bestowed on Henry VIII by the Pope and was never relinquished when Henry broke away from Rome?

   Defender of the Faith

5. English and Latin were two of three languages spoken by Henry VIII. Name the third language.

   French

6. Henry VIII imposed a tax on what part of the body, although he himself was exempt from the rule?

   Beards

7. Lasting 6 months and 3 days before it was annulled, to whom was Henry VIII married for the shortest time?

   Anne of Cleves

8. Which book did Henry VIII authorise for reading out loud in church?

   (Great) Bible

9. Shipbuilding was an important investment for Henry VIII. Which boat did he name after his sister?

   Mary Rose

10. Who succeeded Henry VIII to the throne?

    Edward VI

QUIZ 6: ROYALS IN SPORT

Questions on a range of royal sporting activities.

1. Who was the first member of the Royal Family to participate in the Olympic Games?

    Princess Anne

2. The racing colours of Queen Elizabeth II are purple and red with gold braiding. What colour is the cap?

    Black with a Gold Fringe

3. Which member of the Royal Family instigated the Invictus Games?

    Prince Harry

4. Who became President of the All England Lawn Tennis and Croquet Club in 1969?

    Prince Michael, Duke of Kent

5. Sometimes called the "sport of kings", which racquet sport did Henry VIII play at Hampton Palace?

    Real Tennis

6. Which June sporting event was started by Queen Anne in 1711 and is attended every year by members of the Royal Family?

    Royal Ascot

7. Which Royal Family member was a captain of the England rugby team?

    Mike Tindall

8. What was given to the Royal Family in 1886, starting a royal interest in this recreational sport?

    Racing Pigeons

9. Who became President of the Football Association in May 2006?

    Prince William

10. Which member of the Royal Family won a Silver medal at the 2012 Olympic Games in London?

    Zara Phillips

QUIZ 7: ROYAL LITERATURE

*Name the royal authors of these published books.
The date of publication is in brackets.*

1. "The Old Man of Lochnagar"
   Prince Charles

2. "Elizabeth R: A Photographic Celebration of 40 Years"
   Earl of Lichfield

3. "The Defence of the Seven Sacraments" (1521)
   Henry VIII

4. "Budgie the Helicopter"
   Duchess of York

5. "Harmony: A New Way of Looking at Our World" (2010)
   Prince Charles

6. "The Adventures of Alice Laselles"
   Queen Victoria

7. "Competition Carriage Driving" (1982)
   Prince Philip

8. "Agnes Sorel: Mistress of Beauty"
   Princess Michael of Kent

9. "Daemonology" (1597)
   King James VI of Scotland

10. "The Environmental Revolution" (1978)
    Prince Philip

QUIZ 8: THE ELIZABETHAN ERA

Test your knowledge of events during the reign of Elizabeth I.

1. Henry VIII was the father of Elizabeth I. Who was her mother?
   Anne Boleyn

2. Which naval fleet was defeated by the English in 1588?
   Spanish Armada

3. During the Elizabethan era the government was made up of the monarch, parliament and which other council?
   Privy Council

4. Sir Walter Raleigh is famed for bringing which vegetable back to Europe from his explorations?
   Potato

5. Which Elizabethan playhouse, situated on the River Thames, was associated with William Shakespeare?
   The Globe

6. In 1562, Elizabeth I was very ill from which infectious disease?
   Smallpox

7. Which local English language could Elizabeth I speak, a language that is still spoken by about 2,000 people?
   Cornish

8. What did over 20,000 people in London die from in 1563?
   Bubonic Plague/The Black Death

9. Elizabethan laws dictated what clothes people could wear. What were only Royal people allowed to wear on their cuffs?
   Ermine Fur

10. Who was the first Englishman to circumnavigate the globe on a ship called "The Golden Hind"?
    Sir Francis Drake

QUIZ 9: THE ROYAL HOUSEHOLDS

*These questions are about the Royal Households who are responsible for supporting members of the Royal Family.
Select your answer from the multiple-choice options.*

1. The Lord Steward and the Lord Chamberlain are two of the three Great Officers of the Household. Who is the third Officer?
Prime Minister/**Master of the Horse**/Private Secretary

2. Which member of the Royal Household can be heard at 9.00 am every morning?
Master of the Household/Household Dog Walker/**Queen's Piper**

3. Who looks after the Queen's personal finances?
Keeper of the Privy Purse/Chancellor of the Exchequer/Bank Manager

4. Apart from English, in which language might the Queen's approval be given for bills of Parliament?
Latin/**French**/Spanish

5. Approximately, how many phone calls did the Royal Household receive in 2017?
300,000/500,000/**700,000**

6. What is the Crown Equerry responsible for looking after?
Royal Mews/Kensington Palace/Palace Gardens

7. In 2017, approximately how many people attended Garden Parties hosted by the Queen?
30,000/**50,000**/70,000

8. Approximately, how many offices are there in Buckingham Palace?
52/72/**92**

9. Which document is issued every day by the Royal Household?
News Bulletin/**Court Circular**/Staffing List

10. During every State Opening of Parliament, who is taken hostage by the Royal Household?
A Judge/**An MP**/A Bishop

QUIZ 10: ROYAL MUSIC

Questions linked to royalty and music.

1. Who wrote the "Music for the Royal Fireworks"?

   Handel

2. Which patriotic song was first performed publicly in 1745?

   National Anthem

3. The composer of "Pomp and Circumstance" became "Master of the King's Music" in 1924. Who was he?

   Edward Elgar

4. Which London concert venue was dedicated to a prince following his death?

   Albert Hall

5. In 2000, Prince Charles revived the appointment of which musician to the Royal Court?

   Harpist

6. According to the nursery rhyme, who "marched his men to the top of the hill and he marched them down again"?

   The Grand Old Duke of York

7. Opened in 1892, which performing arts venue in Covent Garden was formerly a theatre?

   Royal Opera House

8. Who played his guitar on the roof of Buckingham Palace as part of the Golden Jubilee celebrations in 2002?

   Brian May

9. What did the Queen receive following the recording sales of "Party At The Palace", the first member of the Royal Family to be given this music honour?

   Gold Disc

10. The music for which planet from Holst's "The Planets" was used at the coronation of Queen Elizabeth II and is also the tune for the hymn "I Vow to Thee, My Country?"

    Jupiter

QUIZ 11: THE EDWARDIAN ERA

Each question is about an event that occurred during the Edwardian era.

1. In which year did Edward VII become king?
   1901

2. In 1908, which sporting event was held in London?
   Summer Olympic Games

3. Who, with her daughters, founded the Women's Social and Political Union in 1902?
   Emmeline Pankhurst

4. Name the successful children's book written by Beatrix Potter and published by Frederick Warne & Co. in 1902.
   The Tale of Peter Rabbit

5. Which shopkeeper opened a store in Oxford Street in 1909, and put cosmetics on open display for the first time?
   Gordon Selfridge

6. French aviator, Louis Blériot, invented an aircraft that was used to successfully cross which body of water for the first time in 1909?
   English Channel

7. Which playwright wrote "Man and Superman" and "Pygmalion" during the Edwardian era?
   George Bernard Shaw

8. What prizes, still awarded today, were presented for the first time in 1901 for work in the fields of literature, medicine, physics, chemistry and peace?
   Nobel Prizes

9. Who, in 1905, proposed a "Theory of Relativity"?
   Albert Einstein

10. Which part of the world was reached for the first time by explorer Roald Amundsen in 1911?
    South Pole

QUIZ 12: BY ROYAL APPOINTMENT

Answer these questions about Royal Warrants, given in recognition of those who have supplied goods or services to the Royal Household.

1. What is the minimum length of time a trader has to supply goods or services to the Royal Household before being considered for a Royal Warrant?

    5 Years

2. A Royal Warrant can be granted by the Queen, the Duke of Edinburgh and which other Royal member?

    Prince of Wales

3. Which dairy product is associated with Royal Warrant holders "Paxton and Whitfield"?

    Cheese

4. Approximately, how many suppliers held Royal Warrants in 2017?

    800

5. Which purveyor of baked beans and tomato ketchup has a Royal Warrant?

    Heinz

6. What type of hat did Lock & Co., hat suppliers to the Royal Household, create?

    Bowler Hat

7. After how many years does a Royal Warrant have to be renewed?

    5 Years

8. Barrow & Gale, Royal Warrant Holders, produce special purses traditionally given out by the Queen just before Easter Sunday. What name is given to the silver coins put into the purses?

    Maundy Money

9. In the 18th century the "Royal Bug-Taker" was responsible for getting rid of what type of bug?

    Bed Bugs

10. What is the name of the Piccadilly grocery store that is often referred to as the "Queen's grocer"?

    Fortnum and Mason

QUIZ 13: ROYAL ANIMALS

Questions about the Royal Family and their love of animals.

1. What type of dog was created by the Queen?
   Dorgi

2. The Queen, together with the Worshipful Company of Vintners and the Worshipful Company of Dyers, own all British swans. What is the name of the annual ceremony to count the swans on the River Thames?
   Swan Upping

3. Which animals reside in the main hall at Balmoral Castle?
   Bats

4. What was the name of the horse with which Zara Philips won a number of equestrian gold medals?
   Toytown

5. Which exotic animal was given to the Queen and Princess Margaret by their second cousin, Lord Mountbatten?
   Chameleon

6. Belonging to the Duke and Duchess of Cambridge, what breed of dog is "Lupo"?
   Cocker Spaniel

7. The term "Fishes Royal" refers to ownership by the Queen of any whale, porpoise, dolphin or sturgeon that is caught or lands within how many miles of the British coastline?
   3 Miles

8. The Queen's horse, "Estimate" won the Ascot Gold Cup in 2013. As the Queen normally presents the Cup, who did the honours?
   Prince Andrew, Duke of York

9. In 1979, Prince Charles came third in a race at the Royal International Horse Show. What type of animal was he riding?
   Camel

10. Which animal is being reinstituted on the Balmoral estate?
    Red Squirrel

QUIZ 14: ROYAL VEHICLES

How does the Royal Family travel around?

1. What is the name of the boat that was often used by the Royal Family for both State visits and for family holidays?
   Royal Yacht Britannia

2. The Queen is the only person in Britain who is not required to have a driving licence. What else is not needed on any car that the Queen drives?
   Number Plate

3. On a State visit to Tuvalu, the Queen and Prince Philip travelled on what kind of water-craft?
   Canoe

4. Launched in 2014, what name has been given to the largest aircraft carrier belonging to the Royal Navy?
   HMS Queen Elizabeth

5. Which vehicle did Prince Philip buy in 1999 and has been used to transport the Prince around London?
   London Taxi Cab/Metrocab

6. Who was the first British monarch to travel by train?
   Queen Victoria

7. During World War II, the Queen joined the Women's Auxillary Territorial Service and trained as a mechanic and driver of which army vehicle?
   Military Truck

8. Where is the Queen's collection of cars stored?
   Royal Mews, Buckingham Palace

9. In 1939, which transport system did the Queen and her sister Princess Margaret use for the first time?
   London Underground

10. What vehicle did the Queen use for travelling to Westminster Abbey for her coronation?
    Gold State Coach

QUIZ 15: QUEEN VICTORIA

A variety of questions on the life of Queen Victoria.

1. How many children did Queen Victoria and Prince Albert have?
   9

2. "The Works of Industry of All Nations" were displayed in Hyde Park for almost six months in 1851. What was the occasion called?
   The Great Exhibition/Crystal Palace Exhibition

3. At what age did Victoria become Queen of the United Kingdom?
   18 Years

4. What type of toy did Queen Victoria make as a child?
   Peg Dolls

5. Which British medal was introduced in 1856 to reward acts of courage during the Crimean War, and remains the highest accolade of bravery today?
   Victoria Cross

6. What was Queen Victoria's first name?
   Alexandrina

7. Queen Victoria presented a gift made from the timbers of HMS Resolute to President Rutherford B. Hayes. It has been used in the Oval Office by many US Presidents. What was the gift?
   Desk

8. Which object did Queen Victoria possess that was bulletproof and lined with chainmail?
   Umbrella

9. What did Queen Victoria wear on her wedding day that set a trend for brides that still exists today?
   White Wedding Dress

10. Queen Victoria was the first British monarch to sit for what sort of picture?
    Photograph

QUIZ 16: STATE VISITS

Her Majesty Queen Elizabeth II has undertaken many state visits, both as a host and as a visitor to other countries. These questions are about state visits, both home and abroad.

1. What does the Queen not need when travelling abroad?

    Passport

2. During a State visit in 1982, which American President did the Queen go horse riding with through Windsor Park?

    Ronald Reagan

3. Which country has been visited the most times by the Queen?

    Canada

4. In 1983, which 'crooner' organised a royal tribute on the sound stage at 20th Century Fox in Hollywood?

    Frank Sinatra

5. Which was the first country that the Queen made a State visit to?

    Norway

6. On a 1994 tour, where did the Queen watch the Bolshoi Ballet perform "Giselle"?

    Moscow

7. In 1986, the Queen became the first British monarch to visit which country?

    China

8. During a tour of Brazil in 1968, which footballer impressed the Queen when she watched a match at the Maracanã Stadium?

    Pelé

9. King Bhumipol and Queen Sirikit made a State visit to the United Kingdom in 1960. Which country were they from?

    Thailand

10. In 1990, part of a state visit was a walk along a wooden pathway looking at hot springs and other geothermal activity. Which country was the Queen visiting?

    Iceland

QUIZ 17: ROYAL FOOD

A variety of questions linking royalty and food.

1. Chicken, herbs, spices and mayonnaise are the main ingredients for a dish created in 1953. Name the recipe.
   Coronation Chicken

2. Which gift does the Queen customarily give to staff members at Christmas?
   Christmas Pudding

3. Eggs, butter, sugar and flour are used to make this layered cake which has jam in the middle. Name the cake.
   Victoria Sponge/Sandwich

4. What variety of potato is named after a monarch?
   King Edward

5. Which member of the Royal Family had a cider apple named after him on his 21st birthday?
   Prince William

6. Gingerbread and marchpane, a product similar to marzipan, were two favourite sugary treats during the reign of which British monarch?
   Elizabeth I

7. In which Scandinavian country did the Queen eat smoked reindeer at a state banquet?
   Finland

8. Name the pink and yellow cake that is covered in marzipan.
   Battenburg

9. Which popular bread-based food is believed to have been named after an Italian queen?
   Pizza Margherita

10. What flavour is "Queen Mother's cake"?
    Chocolate

QUIZ 18: BRITISH STAMPS

The present day postal service has Royal roots.
Test your knowledge of British mail.

1. The Penny Black was the world's first adhesive stamp. The head of which king or queen is on the Penny Black?
   Queen Victoria

2. Which English monarch introduced the Royal Mail?
   Henry VIII

3. What was the highest value stamp ever issued in Britain?
   £5

4. Which way does the Queen's head face on postage stamps?
   To the left

5. What is different about British stamps from all other postage stamps in the world?
   Do not have the name of the country on them

6. Where would you find the "Court Post Office"?
   Buckingham Palace

7. Who was the first non-royal to appear on UK postage stamps as a commemoration for the 400th anniversary of his birthday?
   William Shakespeare

8. A miniature silhouette of the monarch's head appears on all UK stamps. What appears, in relation to the monarch, on UK post boxes?
   Monarch's Initials

9. What name is given to stamp collecting?
   Philately

10. As one of the commemorative stamps for the Queen's 90th birthday, which member of the Royal Family appeared on a postage stamp at the age of 2 years?
    Prince George

QUIZ 19: ROYAL CASTLES AND PALACES

Questions about Royal residences.

1. Acquired by George III in 1761, which building is the official London residence of the Queen?

    Buckingham Palace

2. In which part of the United Kingdom is the Queen's official residence of Hillsborough Castle?

    Northern Ireland

3. Where was the childhood home of Elizabeth, the Queen Mother, and birthplace of Princess Margaret?

    Glamis Castle

4. Osborne House was a former Royal residence of Queen Victoria. On which island can it be found?

    Isle of Wight

5. The cast of which West End show performed at Windsor Castle during a state visit by President Jacques Chirac?

    Les Misérables

6. Which palace was given to Henry VIII as a gift from Cardinal Wolsey?

    Hampton Court Palace

7. In London, where is the official residence of the Prince of Wales?

    Clarence House

8. Which castle is frequented by the Royal Family for summer holidays?

    Balmoral

9. Henry VIII was born in the Palace of Placentia, as was Queen Elizabeth I. In which Royal London borough is the Palace of Placentia?

    Greenwich

10. What is the name of the country house in Norfolk where the Royal Family traditionally spends Christmas?

    Sandringham House

QUIZ 20: THE REIGN OF ELIZABETH II

Her Majesty, Queen Elizabeth II has been on the throne for over 60 years. These questions are on events that have occurred during that time.

1. Who broke the four-minute mile barrier in 1954?

    Roger Banister

2. Which car appeared for the first time in 1959?

    Austin Mini

3. What trophy did an English sports team win in 1966?

    Football World Cup

4. What financial change was launched in the UK in 1971?

    Decimal Currency

5. In 1977, which horse won the Grand National for the third time?

    Red Rum

6. On 1st January, 1985, which electronic device was used publicly for the first time by Ernie Wise?

    Mobile Phone

7. What did Tim Berniers-Lee invent in 1989?

    World Wide Web

8. What linked England and France in 1994?

    Channel Tunnel

9. How old was the Queen Mother on 4th August, 2000?

    100 Years

10. Which anniversary did the Queen celebrate on 7th February, 2017?

    Sapphire Jubilee (65 Years as Monarch)

Quizmaster Section 3: BE YOUR OWN QUIZMASTER!

Helpful hints for running your own quiz.

Quizmaster Helpful Hints

Hint 1 Decide on a maximum number of people per team. This makes the competition fairer for everyone taking part.

Hint 2 State clearly at the beginning of the quiz that the Quizmaster's decision is final regarding answers given.

Hint 3 Decide in advance whether as Quizmaster you will accept one part of a name only, e.g. surname. You could give a ½ point for one part of the name. Let the teams know the rule you have set before you start.

Hint 4 Consider using 'Jokers'. Each team has a joker that they can decide to use in advance of a round starting. Their score for that round will then be doubled. This adds another level of interest to the competition.

Hint 5 Allow spelling mistakes. Make it clear that providing the words can be read as the correct answer, then points will be given.

Hint 6 Think about time allowance per question and let teams know this at the start of the quiz.

Hint 7 Have plenty of spare pens or pencils ready to supply teams as necessary.

Hint 8 Sample quiz answer sheets are available on the next page. Please feel free to copy these.

Hint 9　　　Let the teams choose their own team names. This is an icebreaker and can produce some very funny results! To encourage the teams, you could offer a price for the most original or funniest team name.

Hint 10　　Read each question out twice. Be clear when talking and make sure everyone can hear you. Try to make each question sound interesting! Allow approximately 10 seconds for teams to write their answer down before reading out the next question.

Quizmaster Sample Answer Sheet

Team Name ....

Round ....

Answers

1. ....

2. ....

3. ....

4. ....

5. ....

6. ....

7. ....

8. ....

9. ....

10. ....

THANKS

My thanks go to everyone who has encouraged me to publish quizzes and who has endured the endless listening to questions and being expected to provide answers; your support has been my motivation.

My biggest thanks go to my mum for being the original inspiration behind my love of all things quizzical.

Acknowledgement

Crown icon made by Nikita Golubev from www.flaticon.com

MORE TITLES BY GINNY HILL

Other quizzes from the Quizmaster series:

Music
Christmas
Food and Drink
Months of the Year
Scotland
USA
Seasons
Homes
Love
Colours
The Seaside

Travelling? Then try …

On the Go!
Travel Games for Everyone

By
Ginny Hill

Printed in Great Britain
by Amazon